# MEET SHAI GILGEOUS-ALEXANDER

MARGARET J. GOLDSTEIN

Lerner Publications ◆ Minneapolis

Lerner Publications Company
An imprint of Lerner Publishing Group, Inc.
241 First Avenue North
Minneapolis, MN 55401 USA

For reading levels and more information, look up this title at www.lernerbooks.com.

Main body text set in Aptifer Slab LT Pro. Typeface provided by Linotype AG.

**Editor:** Annie Zheng

**Library of Congress Cataloging-in-Publication Data**

Names: Goldstein, Margaret J., author.
Title: Meet Shai Gilgeous-Alexander : Oklahoma City Thunder superstar / Margaret J. Goldstein.
Description: Minneapolis : Lerner Publications, [2025] | Series: Lerner sports. Sports VIPs | Includes bibliographical references and index. | Audience: Ages 7–11 years | Audience: Grades 4–6 | Summary: "In 2023–2024, Shai Gilgeous-Alexander finished fourth in the NBA in scoring with 31.4 points per game. Readers will enjoy learning more about the Oklahoma Thunder City guard's life on and off the court"— Provided by publisher.
Identifiers: LCCN 2024024097 (print) | LCCN 2024024098 (ebook) | ISBN 9798765649299 (lib. bdg.) | ISBN 9798765662496 (pbk.) | ISBN 9798765658673 (epub)
Subjects: LCSH: Gilgeous-Alexander, Shai—Juvenile literature. | Guards (Basketball)—United States—Biography—Juvenile literature. | Basketball players—Canada—Biography—Juvenile literature. | Oklahoma City Thunder (Basketball team)—Juvenile literature. | Basketball—Canada—Toronto—History—Juvenile literature. | Basketball—Oklahoma—Oklahoma City—History—Juvenile literature.
Classification: LCC GV884.G49 G65 2025 (print) | LCC GV884.G49 (ebook) | DDC 796.332092 [B]—dc23/eng/20240706

LC record available at https://lccn.loc.gov/2024024097
LC ebook record available at https://lccn.loc.gov/2024024098

Manufactured in the United States of America
1-1011069-53541-9/4/2024

# TABLE OF CONTENTS

# BUZZER-BEATER

The Oklahoma City Thunder needed a basket. For most of the December 2023 game, they had trailed the Denver Nuggets, the defending National Basketball Association (NBA) champs. But late in the fourth quarter, the Thunder finally closed the gap.

The Nuggets led 117–116, with just seconds left to play. Moving down the court with the basketball, Thunder point guard Shai Gilgeous-Alexander dribbled slowly at first. Then he broke into a flurry of action.

## FAST FACTS

**DATE OF BIRTH:** July 12, 1998
**POSITION:** point guard
**LEAGUE:** NBA

**PROFESSIONAL HIGHLIGHTS:** named an NBA All-Star twice; came in second in 2024 Most Valuable Player (MVP) voting; was second in the league in points and first in steals in 2023–2024

**PERSONAL HIGHLIGHTS:** has a child named Ares; is famous for his eye-catching clothing; is the son of an Olympic track athlete

Gilgeous-Alexander drives the ball past a Denver Nuggets defender.

He charged forward, stopped, surged forward again, spun around, and shot over the outstretched arms of a defender. The ball swished through the net for two points. The clock ticked down to zero. The job was done. Oklahoma won the game 118–117.

Gilgeous-Alexander showed his greatness in that game and many others. Playing in his sixth year in the

NBA, he was leading his team to the top of the Western Conference standings and approaching superstar status. Luka Doncic, a point guard with the Dallas Mavericks, called him "one of the best players in the world."

Thunder coach Mark Daigneault added his praise for Gilgeous-Alexander: "There is no one I'd rather have on our team."

Gilgeous-Alexander shoots over the outstretched arm of a Nuggets player.

# CHAPTER 1

# KID'S STUFF

Shaivonte (Shai) Aician Gilgeous-Alexander was born in Toronto, Canada. He grew up in the nearby town of Hamilton (*pictured*). His parents, Charmaine Gilgeous and Vaughn Alexander, divorced when he was young. Shai and his little brother, Thomasi, lived with their mom. But they saw their dad often.

One of Shai's best friends was his cousin Nickeil Alexander-Walker. Their families lived near each other. The two boys loved to play sports together, especially basketball. Shai hoped to someday play in the NBA.

When Shai was six, he started playing with youth basketball clubs. He also played on youth soccer and football teams. His dad coached some of his youth teams.

In 2024, Shai Gilgeous-Alexander (*left*) and Nickeil Alexander-Walker (*right*) both played for Team Canada at the Olympic Games in Paris, France.

In ninth grade, Shai entered St. Thomas More Catholic Secondary School. He played on the school's freshman basketball team, which won the city championship in 2013. He also joined UPLAY Canada, a top youth basketball program. Shai still played with his cousin Nickeil. They had one-on-one games nearly every day.

Shai's parents and coaches thought he needed tougher competition. So they had him switch high schools. At Sir Allan MacNab Secondary School in Hamilton, Shai upped his game. Playing point guard, he was a standout scorer. High school coach Dwayne Washington thought Shai needed even more of a challenge. With Washington's urging, Shai enrolled at Hamilton Heights Christian Academy in Chattanooga, Tennessee.

In 2024, Alexander-Walker played guard for the Minnesota Timberwolves in the NBA.

Nickeil Alexander-Walker was also a promising high school player. Coaches sent him to Hamilton Heights as well. The two cousins moved to Tennessee. They lived in the home of their coach, Zach Ferrell.

Shai was determined to get better. At Hamilton Heights, he put in extra hours at the gym. This hard work paid off on the basketball court. He helped Hamilton Heights win the City of Palms Classic, a high-level high school tournament, in 2015. Many college coaches hoped that Shai would join their team after graduation.

# CHAPTER 2

# WILDCAT

Gilgeous-Alexander graduated from high school in 2017. Many colleges offered him scholarships. He chose the University of Kentucky, coached by John Calipari. The Kentucky Wildcats were one of the best teams in college basketball.

The 2017 team was loaded with talent. At first, Gilgeous-Alexander was not a starter. He sat on the bench early in games. The coach sent him in when other players needed a break.

It soon became clear that Gilgeous-Alexander was just as good as the starters, if not better. In game after game, he came through with steals, assists, and baskets. Midway through the season, Calipari made him a starter.

Gilgeous-Alexander dribbles the ball past a Kansas Jayhawks defender in a November 2017 game.

As the season went on, he got better and better. He stepped up when the team needed him. For instance, in a game against Vanderbilt University, the Wildcats looked shaky. Partway through the second half, they trailed by 14 points.

Then Gilgeous-Alexander sprang into action. With the clock ticking down, he poured in basket after basket. The game went into overtime and ended with a Wildcats victory. Gilgeous-Alexander shot a career-high 30 points in that game.

Gilgeous-Alexander cutting through Vanderbilt's defense with the ball in 2018

Gilgeous-Alexander scored 29 points against Tennessee in the 2018 Southeastern Conference tournament.

In the 2018 Southeastern Conference tournament, he averaged 21 points, 6.7 rebounds, and five assists per game. When Kentucky faced Tennessee in the tournament championship, Gilgeous-Alexander again went into high gear. He scored 29 points that night. The Wildcats won the game 77–72, and Gilgeous-Alexander was named the tournament's MVP.

He worked just as hard off the court. He did extra early

Gilgeous-Alexander talking to reporters in college

morning workouts with an assistant coach. He pushed himself in the weight room and studied game videos. “He’s probably our hardest worker,” said Kenny Payne, then associate head coach of the Wildcats. “He’s been a dream to coach.”

Gilgeous-Alexander was just a freshman in college, but basketball coaches thought he was good enough to play in the NBA. He also felt he was ready for the pros. In April 2018, he announced that he would enter the upcoming NBA draft.

# CHAPTER 3

# BIG-LEAGUE BALL

At the 2018 NBA Draft, the Charlotte Hornets selected Gilgeous-Alexander with the 11th overall pick. The Hornets then traded him to the Los Angeles Clippers.

Gilgeous-Alexander's dreams of playing in the NBA were about to come true. Talking to reporters after the draft he said, "Getting drafted into the NBA is the best feeling in the world."

Only 20 years old, Gilgeous-Alexander was surrounded by older, more experienced players on the Clippers. But he soon showed that he belonged. He began the 2018 season as the team's backup point guard. But he played well and

Holding up his new jersey, Gilgeous-Alexander (*second from left*) is introduced as one of the Clippers' newest players.

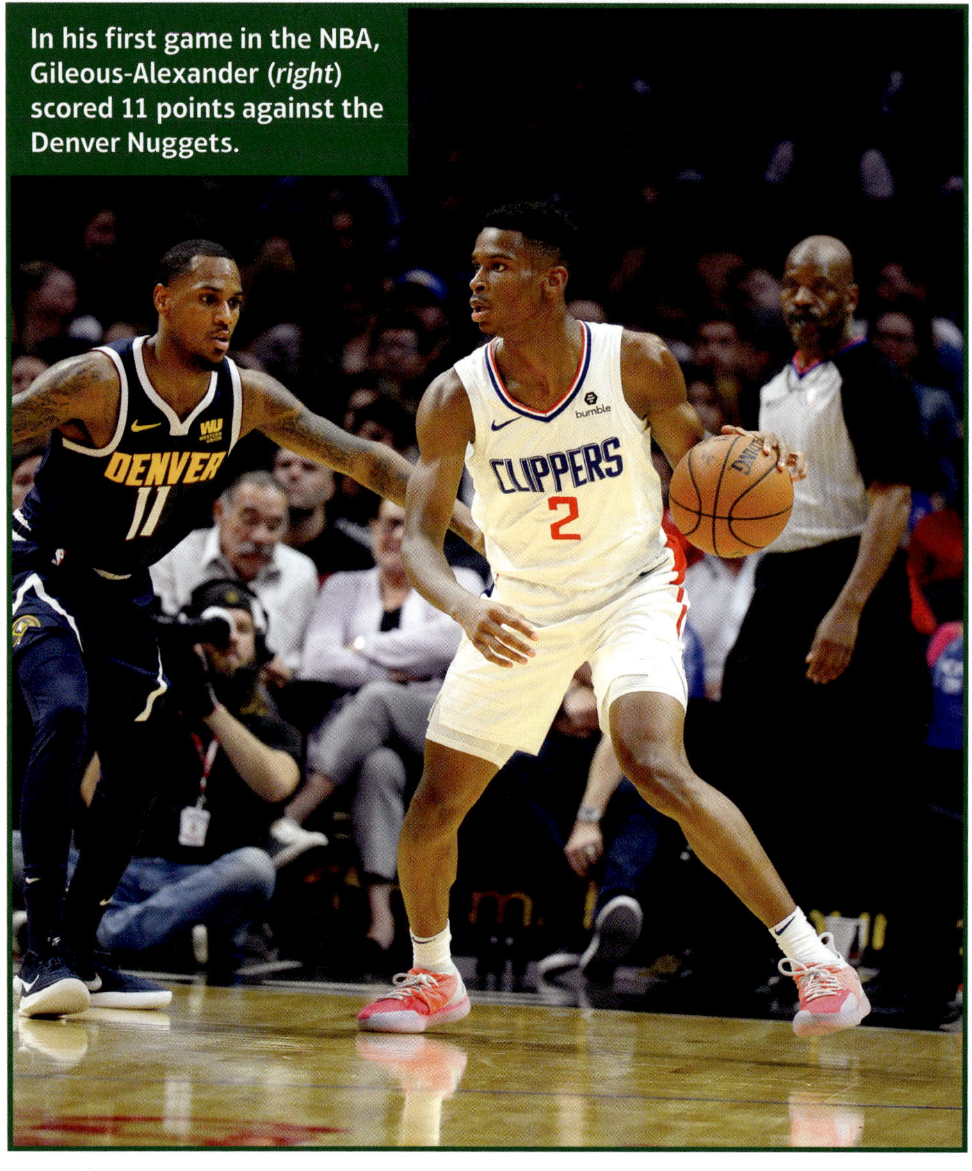


In his first game in the NBA, Gileous-Alexander (*right*) scored 11 points against the Denver Nuggets.

by the 10th game he had earned the starting spot. Among teams with a winning record, he scored more points and played more minutes than any other rookie that year.

Gilgeous-Alexander was a rising star, but Clippers management believed a different group of players would help the team win a championship. In 2019, the Clippers traded Gilgeous-Alexander to the Oklahoma Thunder. He was surprised to be traded, but he took the change in stride.

## SUPER SPORTS SCOOP

Gilgeous-Alexander is famous for more than just basketball. He's also known for his colorful, eye-catching clothing. He describes his look as streetwear mixed with high fashion. In 2022, the men's magazine *GQ* named him the Most Stylish Man of the Year.

Gilgeous-Alexander drives the ball past Jarrett Culver of the Minnesota Timberwolves in a January 2020 game.

With the Thunder, Gilgeous-Alexander continued his impressive play. He had his first NBA triple-double in January 2020. The season was cut short due to the COVID-19 pandemic, but Gilgeous-Alexander used the time off well. He worked out at home with weights. He did push-ups and pull-ups. When he came back for the next season, he was stronger than ever.

He continued to put up big numbers, but he hurt his foot in March 2021. He sat out for the rest of the season. The following year brought another disappointment. This time, in March 2022, his season ended with an ankle injury.

# CHAPTER 4

# ALL-STAR

In 2022–2023, his fifth season in the NBA, Gilgeous-Alexander became one of the league's top shooters. He averaged 31.4 points per game. In December 2022, he scored a career-high 44 points in a game against New Orleans. He scored another 44 points against Portland in February 2023.

That same month, the NBA named him to the 2023 All-Star team, an honor given to the best players in the league. When the regular season ended, a group of sports journalists and broadcasters voted for the league MVP. Gilgeous-Alexander came in fifth.

Gilgeous-Alexander playing for Team Canada in the 2023 Basketball World Cup

The Thunder had 40 wins and 42 losses in 2022–2023. But 2023–2024 was a big improvement. Gilgeous-Alexander and his teammates, including Jalen Williams and Chet Holmgren, had 57 wins and 25 losses that season. The team took first place in the Western Conference standings.

Gilgeous-Alexander racked up big numbers of his own. He was second in the league in total points in 2024 and tied for first in steals. He was again named to the All-Star team. In the 2024 MVP voting, he came in second.

In 2024, the Thunder made the playoffs for the first time in four years. In the first round, they beat the New Orleans Pelicans. But the powerful Dallas Mavericks knocked them out in round two. Gilgeous-Alexander was sad to see his playoff run end. But he had a lot to look forward to.

Gilgeous-Alexander attempting a shot against the New Orleans Pelicans in the 2024 playoffs

Gilgeous-Alexander preparing to shoot in a playoff game against the Dallas Mavericks

He and his wife, Hailey Summers, had a baby boy, Ares, born in April 2024. He also had a deal with Converse to endorse its athletic shoes. And of course he had more basketball ahead. At the end of the 2024 season, a reporter asked him what would make the next five years a success. He answered, "If we win an NBA championship."

# SHAI GILGEOUS-ALEXANDER CAREER STATS

GAMES:

**386**

POINTS:

**8,810**

ASSISTS:

**1,876**

REBOUNDS:

**1,832**

STEALS:

**535**



Stats are accurate through the 2023–2024 NBA regular season.

# GLOSSARY

**assist:** a pass to a teammate that leads to a score

**conference:** one of several parts of a sports league. Teams in a conference play most of their games against one another.

**COVID-19 pandemic:** a disease outbreak that spread around the world starting in late 2019

**draft:** when teams take turns choosing new players

**endorse:** to promote a company by using or wearing its products and appearing in its advertisements

**overtime:** extra playing time added to a game to break a tie

**point guard:** a player whose job is to score and to set up scoring plays for teammates

**rookie:** a first-year player

**scholarship:** money provided to pay for a student's education

**trade:** to transfer a player to another team in exchange for one or more other players, future draft picks, or money

**triple-double:** having double-digit totals in three categories out of five (points, rebounds, assists, blocks, and steals) in a single game

# SOURCE NOTES


7 Louis Pavlakos, "Luka Doncic Calls Shai Gilgeous-Alexander 'One of the Best Players in the World,'" Complex CA, September 7, 2023, https://www.complex.com/sports/a/louispavlakos/luka-doncic-praises-shai-gilgeous-alexander.

7 Rylan Stiles, "Mark Daigneault Weighs in on Shai Gilgeous-Alexander's MVP Case," *Sports Illustrated*, April 19, 2024, https://www.si.com/nba/thunder/news/nba-award-shai-gilgeous-alexander-mvp-daigneault.

17 Brian Bennett, "When Shai Gilgeous-Alexander Got It Going, so Did Kentucky," Athletic, March 21, 2018, https://theathletic.com/282101/2018/03/21/when-shai-gilgeous-alexander-got-it-going-so-did-kentucky/.

19 "Shai Gilgeous-Alexander NBA Draft 2018 Interview," YouTube video, 0:40, posted by LA Clippers, June 21, 2018, https://www.youtube.com/watch?v=sOMeQvEbjf0.

27 Rylan Stiles, "'Capable of Anything': Shai Gilgeous-Alexander Gets Candid with NBA Today about Thunder Title Chances," *Sports Illustrated*, March 7, 2024, https://www.si.com/nba/thunder/news/okc-thunder-shai-gilgeous-alexander-championship-capable.

# LEARN MORE

CBC Kids News: Watch—Five Things about Canadian NBA Player Shai Gilgeous-Alexander
https://www.cbc.ca/kidsnews/post/watch-5-things-about-canadian-nba-player-shai-gilgeous-alexander

Giedd, Steph. *Oklahoma City Thunder.* Mendota Heights, MN: Press Box Books, 2024.

Lowe, Alexander. *G.O.A.T. Basketball Point Guards*. Minneapolis: Lerner Publications, 2023.

Mahoney, Brian. *Oklahoma City Thunder.* Minneapolis: SportsZone, 2023.

*National Geographic Kids*: Bonkers about Basketball
https://www.natgeokids.com/uk/kids-club/entertainment/general-entertainment/bonkers-about-basketball/

*Sports Illustrated Kids*: Basketball
https://www.sikids.com/basketball

# INDEX



# PHOTO ACKNOWLEDGMENTS

Image credits: AP Photo/Kyle Phillips, p. 4; AP Photo/David Zalubowski, p. 6; Matthew Stockman/Getty Images, p. 7; Wirestock Creators/Shutterstock, p. 8; Ethan Miller/Getty Images, p. 9; David Berding/Getty Images, p. 11; AP Photo/James Crisp, pp. 12, 17; AP Photo/Robin Alam/Icon Sportswire, p. 13; Michael Reaves/Getty Images, p. 14; Andy Lyons/Getty Images, p. 15; AP Photo/John Locher, p. 18; AP Photo/Damian Dovarganes, p. 19; Robert Laberge/Getty Images, p. 20; AP Photo/Jim Mone, p. 22; Megan Briggs/Getty Images, p. 23; Meng Yongmin/Xinhua/Getty Images, p. 24; AP Photo/Gerald Herbert, p. 28; AP Photo/Tony Gutierrez, p. 29.

Cover: AP Photo/Matt Patterson.